20th Century Inventions
TELECOMMUNICATIONS

Chris Oxlade

WAYLAND

20th Century Inventions

AIRCRAFT

COMPUTERS

THE INTERNET

LASERS

NUCLEAR POWER

ROCKETS AND SPACECRAFT

SATELLITES

TELECOMMUNICATIONS

Cover and title page: A large dish antenna in southern Australia beams radio signals up to a communication satellite in orbit around Earth.

Series editor: Philippa Smith
Book editor: Paul Bennett
Series designer: Tim Mayer
Book designer: Malcolm Walker of Kudos Design
Cover designer: Dennis Day

First published in 1996 by Wayland Publishers Limited,
61 Western Road, Hove, East Sussex BN3 1JD, England

British Library Cataloguing in Publication Data
Oxlade, Chris
    Telecommunicatons. – (Twentieth century inventions)
    1. Telecommunications – Juvenile literature
    I. Title
    621.3'82

ISBN 0 7502 1793 6

Typeset by Malcolm Walker of Kudos Design
Printed and bound in Italy by G. Canale & C.S.p.A., Turin

Picture acknowledgements
Svend Erik Andersen 41; Mary Evans Picture Library 18, 20; Eye Ubiquitous 14/Chris Bland, 21/Paul Seheult, 23/Skjold, 24 (bottom)/Paul Seheult, 29 (both)/Paul Seheult; The Image Bank 4/David N. Hamilton, 5/Weinberg and Clark, 11 (top)/ D. Sarraute, 11 (bottom)/Tim Bieber, 26/A.A. Boccaccio, 35 (top)/Chris Close, 35 (bottom)/Steve Dunwell, 36/Alan Becker, 38/Kay Chernush, 39/Steve Niedorf; Science Photo Library front cover and title page/Dr Jeremy Burgess, back cover and contents page/Tony Craddock, 8 (top)/Library of Congress, 15/NASA, 19, 25/John Mead, 27/Julian Baum, 31/Philippe Plailly, 32/Hank Morgan, 40/Phillippe Plailly/Eurelios, 42/Phillippe Plailly; Tony Stone Worldwide 10/ Don Smetzer, 37/Terry Vine; ZEFA 12, 17, 33, 45. Artwork by Tim Benké, Top Draw (Tableau). All other pictures Wayland Picture Library.

20th Century Inventions
CONTENTS

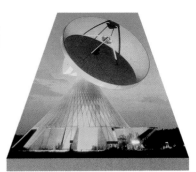

WHAT ARE TELECOMMUNICATIONS?

When you make a telephone call or send a fax message you are using telecommunications. The word telecommunications means sending information between two places along wires, or optical fibres, or by radio waves. The information can be almost anything – voices, music, pictures, words or computer information (data) – and it arrives at its destination almost immediately.

What would life would be like without telecommunications? There would be no telephones, so you would not be able to chat to your friends at the press of a button. There would be no television (TV), so you would not be able to watch your favourite soap opera in the evening. And there would be no radio, so you would not be able to listen to a live music programme.

Television is one form of telecommunications, and the world's most popular form of entertainment.

Changing the world

Less than 200 years ago, there were no telecommunications at all. Messages were often in the form of handwritten letters, which were delivered by people on foot or on horseback.

Since then, telecommunications have completely changed the way we live and work. They help businesses to run smoothly, and shops to keep their shelves full of the goods we buy. People in different continents are able to talk and work together, and most of our entertainment depends on telecommunications.

Radio communications allow people to talk to one another. Here a pilot speaks to an air-traffic controller during a flight.

The telecommunications network

Telephone calls, faxes, computer data, radio and TV programmes all travel from place to place through a huge system of different kinds of links called the telecommunications network. Some links are local, such as the cable that joins your telephone to your local telephone exchange. Others are international, such as satellite links, which can pass on (relay) information to countries on the other side of the world.

Evidence for the links are all around us. For example, the thin wires strung between telegraph poles carry telephone messages, and the aerials and satellite dishes seen attached to houses receive TV pictures.

A typical communications network, showing how different forms of telecommunications reach our homes.

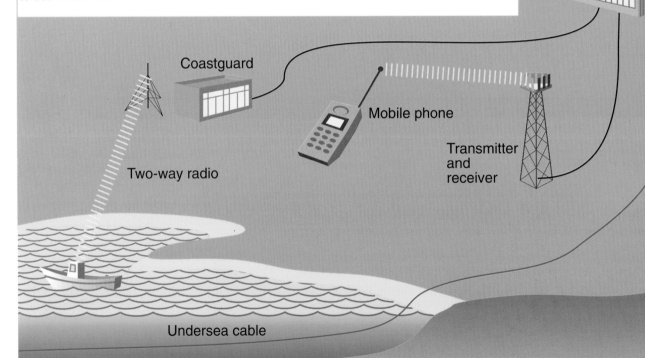

Main telephone exchange

Local telephone exchange

Coastguard

Mobile phone

Two-way radio

Transmitter and receiver

Undersea cable

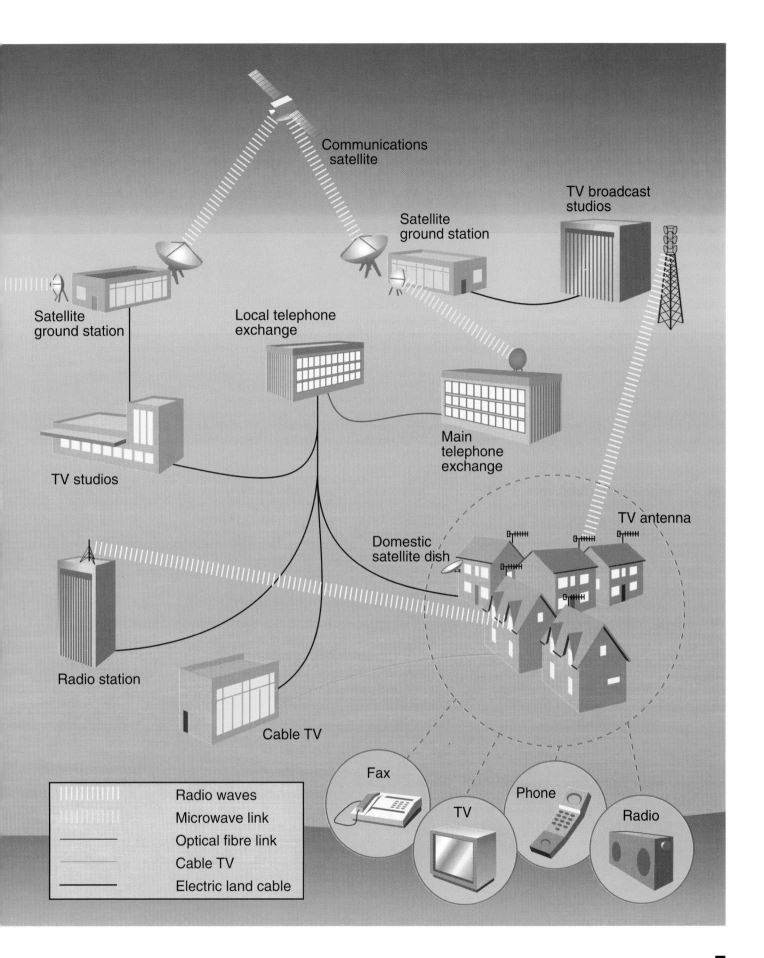

Communications
satellite

TV broadcast
studios

Satellite
ground station

Satellite
ground station

Local telephone
exchange

TV studios

Main
telephone
exchange

TV antenna

Domestic
satellite dish

Radio station

Cable TV

Radio waves	
Microwave link	
Optical fibre link	
Cable TV	
Electric land cable	

Fax

TV

Phone

Radio

TELEPHONES

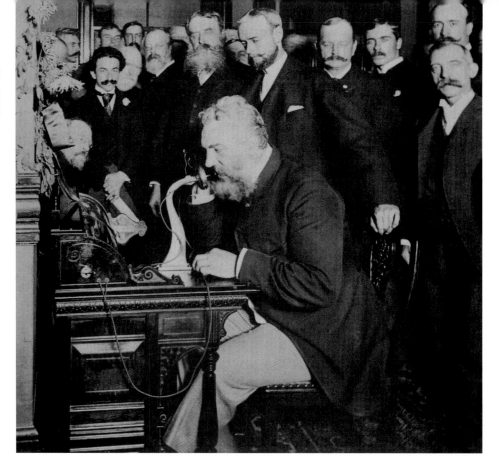

The inventor of the telephone, Alexander Graham Bell, at the opening of the New York to Chicago telephone line in 1892.

Whether at home or at work, telephones help us to keep in touch with one another. They have become such a common part of our everyday lives that we take them almost for granted.

The Scottish-born scientist, Alexander Graham Bell, invented the first working telephone in 1876. He came up with the idea of sending speech along a wire as an electrical signal while he was experimenting with a telegraph machine (see page 18).

A manual telephone exchange in 1910. Dozens of operators were needed to operate the exchange.

In 1878, the first telephone exchange was opened at New Haven in Connecticut in the USA. Just twenty-one local lines were connected to it – it was not possible to speak to people in other parts of the country. To make a call, you pressed a button on your telephone to attract the attention of an 'operator'. The operator asked you who wanted to speak to, and joined the lines together.

By the 1880s, there were many small local exchanges in both the USA and Europe and, in 1884, the first long-distance line was opened between Boston and New York in the USA.

The first automatic telephone exchange – one where machinery rather than an operator connected you to another person – was opened in the USA in 1897. To use an automatic exchange, a telephone with a numbered dial was needed. However, it was not until the 1920s that automatic telephone exchanges became widespread.

Thomas Alva Edison

Edison (1847–1931) was one of the world's greatest inventors. In 1878, he invented a microphone that greatly improved the working of the telephone. The microphone made the person's voice clearer to the listener at the other end of the telephone line.

Before he became famous, Edison was a US telegraph operator. His inventions include the phonograph (the first sound recording machine) and the electric light bulb. He also built the world's first power station.

An engineer checks a circuit board which forms part of a modern electronic telephone exchange.

How telephones work

A telephone receiver or handset has two parts. The mouthpiece (the part you speak into) turns the sound of your voice into an electrical signal which can travel down the telephone line. The earpiece (the part you listen to) turns electrical signals coming up the telephone line back into sound that you can hear.

What happens when you dial

Pressing the numbers on your telephone receiver's keypad sends signals to the telephone network, telling it which of the hundreds of millions of telephones lines in the world you want to be connected to.

Your telephone line is connected to your local telephone exchange. If you are calling a person locally, the exchange connects your line to the other person's telephone line. If you are calling somebody in another town, or another country, the exchange connects your line to another exchange.

Some handsets include the dialling buttons, set between the mouthpiece and earpiece. Many push-button telephones have useful features, such as a memory for storing regularly-used numbers and a button for redialling a number.

Modulation

The electrical signals made by a telephone cannot travel through some parts of the telecommunications network, such as a microwave link or optical fibre. Instead, at the sending station the electrical signal is changed into microwaves or light beams. This process is called modulation. When the microwave or light beam arrives at the receiving station, it is demodulated to get back the electrical signal.

Above **Optical-fibre cables. The hair-thin optical fibres are covered by protective plastic.**

Pulse code modulation

In an optical fibre, signals travel as pulses of light. Before this can happen, the signal must be turned into a code of on and off pulses. This is called pulse code modulation. Once a signal is changed into pulses, it can be sent along a wire as pulses of current, or along an optical fibre as pulses of light.

Left **Telephone engineers testing digital telephone switching equipment at a computerized exchange.**

11

Telephone uses

With a simple telephone call, you can arrange to meet your friends, order food to be delivered, book tickets to the movies, call the doctor or the emergency services and find out about the weather. Office workers use telephones to discuss projects, order supplies, send fax messages and computer data. They can talk to people in their own office building as well as outside. And with telephone answering machines, callers can leave a recorded message if the person they are calling is out.

Emergency services

Telephones are vital in emergency situations. You can contact any of the emergency services – the police, the fire service, the ambulance service or the coastguard – by calling an easy-to-remember number. In Britain the emergency number is 999, in the USA the number is 911 and in Australia it is 000, for example.

As well as the emergency services, there are many other organizations you can call for assistance. If a water pipe bursts or you smell gas, a telephone call will get somebody to help.

An air-sea rescue helicopter winches up a crew member and a casualty. Rescue services are normally called out by telephone.

Videophones

With videophones, you can see the person you are talking to as well as hear them. A videophone contains a tiny video camera and a flat television screen. It sends pictures along the telephone line as well as your voice.

A Japanese man talks to a friend with a videophone linked to the family's television.

Where and when?

The weather forecast, bus or train times to plan your journey, the time the cinema film is being screened – there are telephone information lines for all types of information. Very often the information is in the form of a recorded message.

Some information services allow you choose the message you would like to hear by pressing a number on your telephone or by saying certain words at the right moment.

Intercoms

Intercoms are small telephone systems that are often used in blocks of flats. Visitors call the person they want to see from a telephone at the main door to the block. The person in the flat can unlock the door by pressing a button in the flat. This makes sure that unwanted visitors cannot get into the block.

Telephoning the world

Almost as soon as telephones were invented in 1876, they became a success. Although only the rich could afford one, by 1887, there were over 100,000 telephones around the world, mostly in the cities of North America and Europe.

Telegraph poles were erected to carry telephone lines along streets and distribute them to homes and offices.

Every telephone line was suspended on poles above the street, instead of under them as most are today. By the 1900s, every city was covered in a spider's web of wires. However, with the odd exception, you could not call people in other cities because there were no telephone lines between them.

Linking cities

Sending a weak electrical signal hundreds of kilometres along a wire cable to another city was difficult because the signal gradually lost its strength as it travelled. Telephone companies tried to solve the problem by making the wire cables larger, but this also made the cable expensive to make.

The answer to this problem was the invention of the repeater, a device that became in widespread use in the 1920s. A repeater picks up a weak signal, amplifies it (makes it stronger) and then sends it on its journey. Technological advances like the repeater made it much cheaper for telephone companies to run their networks. This meant cheaper telephone receivers and calls for customers.

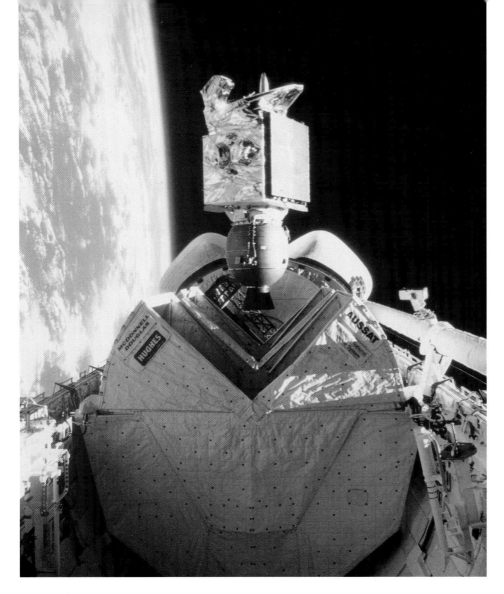

A communications satellite is launched from the bay of Space Shuttle *Discovery*. The small rocket engine takes the satellite up to its high orbit.

Calling abroad

The greatest challenge to telephone engineers in the early part of the twentieth century was to link Europe and North America. In 1927, a radio link was opened for public use. However, a three-minute call on it cost several months' salary. In 1956, engineers laid a submarine telephone cable along the sea-bed between Scotland and Newfoundland in Canada. It could carry eighty-eight telephone calls at the same time.

In 1962, the first communications satellite was launched into space. Submarine cables and satellites can now carry tens of thousands of calls around the world at the same time. Today, it is as cheap to call the other side of the world as it was to call the next town in the 1950s.

Public telephones

Public telephones are useful for making calls when you are out and about. Until the 1960s, public telephones were the only way for most people to make telephone calls. The first coin-operated telephone box was opened in the USA in 1889.

On the move

Most telephones are connected to the telephone network by a telephone line. This is an electrical wire that links the telephone to the local telephone exchange.

But what if you want to make a call from a car, or while out walking in the countryside? You need a mobile phone. Mobile phones are very useful for people who are always on the move or who work outside.

Cellular networks

Mobile phones keep in touch with the telephone network by radio. Spread through the cities and countryside are radio aerials which are owned by mobile telephone companies. Each aerial sends and receives radio signals to and from all the mobile phones in its area. This area is called a cell, which is why mobile phones are also called cellular phones. The aerial is connected to the telephone network through a telephone exchange.

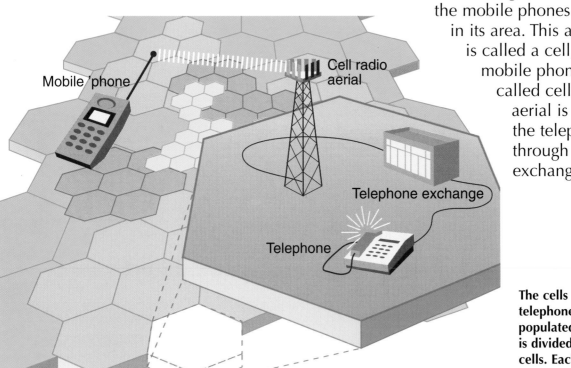

Mobile phone

Cell radio aerial

Telephone exchange

Telephone

The cells of a mobile telephone network. A densely populated area, such as a city, is divided up into many small cells. Each cell has its own aerial connected to the telephone network.

A Samburu warrior makes a call from the Kenyan countryside with a radio telephone.

Portable telephones

Portable telephones let you wander around your home or garden with the telephone receiver. It communicates with the base of the telephone set by radio. The base connects to the telephone line as normal.

Phoning from remote places

In remote areas of the world, such as in a desert or in the middle of an ocean, mobile phones are useless – there are no aerials to connect them to the telephone network. However, with the right equipment, telephones calls can be made with the help of a communications satellites thousands of kilometres up in space. From a cruise liner, you can telephone just as you would from home, and ship telephones have telephone numbers like other telephones.

THE TELEGRAPH SYSTEM

The telegraph was the first telecommunications machine and it worked by sending information between two machines in electrical code. The modern telegraph system – the fax or telex – is used to send business documents around the world. However, fax and electronic mail (see page 39) are now taking over from telex because they are cheaper and easier to use.

How old is the telegraph?

The idea for the telegraph was thought up in the eighteenth century, not long after scientists were beginning to understand how to store and control electricity. The first reliable telegraph machines were built in the 1830s. To send a message, the operators themselves needed to change messages into electronic code.

Machines which did the coding automatically were introduced in the 1850s. By the 1920s, there was a telegraph network stretching right around the world.

An operator using a printing telegraph machine to change a coded message on a paper tape into a printed message on paper.

Samuel Morse

In the 1830s, the US inventor, Samuel Morse (1791–1872), developed a telegraph system. It was designed to use a code of short and long pulses of electric current to represent different letters. The code became known as Morse code.

On the Morse telegraph, the receiving machine was attached to a pen, which left a series of dots and dashes on a moving strip of paper. This allowed the operators to send and receive Morse code.

Above **Samuel Morse.** Morse studied painting in England and was a painter before developing his telegraph system.

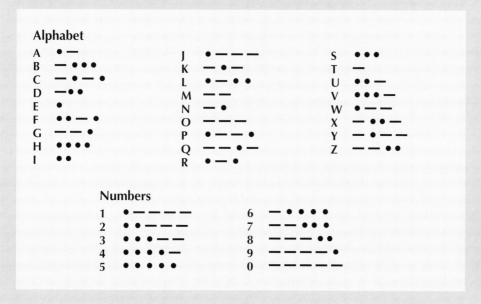

Left **In Morse code, each letter or numeral is represented by a combination of short and long pulses. Other combinations are for punctuation or messages to the operator.**

How did a telegraph work?

The first telegraph machines were very simple. The operator pressed a switch on the machine sending the message, which sent an electric current along a wire to the receiving machine. When it got there, the current made a needle 'twitch'. The operator at the receiving machine knew what the different combinations of twitches of the needles meant, and wrote down the message.

On an automatic telegraph machine, the operator typed the message on a typewriter keyboard. The machine sent the correct electrical pulses automatically. At the other end, another machine printed out the message automatically.

Who uses the telegraph?

The first people to use electrical telegraphs were railway companies. They set up telegraph lines alongside the tracks so that stations could 'talk' to each other. This made the railways much safer because one station could warn another when a train was coming.

Members of the public could visit the telegraph office and pay the railway companies to send telegrams for them. Most people only sent telegrams when they had important news to tell. Telegrams were the only quick way for most people to send a message before there were public telephones.

Who uses telex and fax?

Companies are the main users of telex and fax. Telex is useful because a message can be sent to many different places at the same time. However, with telex, only words can be sent because the message must be typed in on a keyboard. This converts the message into coded pulses for transmission along a wire to a printing receiver, which prints out the message.

A 1930s picture of the Canadian Pacific Railway. As new railroads were built across North America, telegraph lines were set up alongside the tracks.

Sending a fax message

To send a message, a fax machine has to turn the information on a page into an electrical signal which it can send down a telephone line. Inside is a row of hundreds of tiny light sensors. As the page moves past it, the sensors work out in great detail the light and dark parts of the page. In this way, the machine divides the page into thousands of tiny dots, which are either black or white. The machine then sends a signal for each dot down the telephone line.

At the receiving machine, the signals are sent to a row of tiny heating elements. There is one heating element for each light sensor in the sending machine. Heat-sensitive paper moves past the heating elements. Where a dot on the original page was dark, the heating element is turned on. The heat makes the paper turn black, and an image of the original message is printed.

Using a fax machine is as easy as using a telephone. You simply place the message in the machine and dial the number.

With fax, any kind of information that can be put on paper, such as words, drawings and photographs, can be sent. Sending a short fax is cheaper than sending the same information by post (the cost of a telephone call is often cheaper than the cost of postage and packing) and it happens instantly rather than taking a day or so.

RADIO

Radio uses radio waves to send information from one place to another. Radio waves do not need wires to travel along, and they cannot be seen. They can travel through the air and through space, and arrive almost instantly. Radio makes communication of all sorts much quicker and easier. It forms links in the telephone network, makes mobile phones possible, improves safety at sea and in the air, and allows people in remote areas talk to each other. Broadcast radio keeps us entertained and informed.

Guglielmo Marconi

Guglielmo Marconi (1874–1937) was an Italian radio pioneer. He started experimenting in Italy in 1894, but moved to the Britain in 1896, where he succeeded in sending long-distance radio signals. Marconi won the Nobel Prize for Physics in 1909.

Who invented radio?

Nobody really invented radio waves. The fact that radio waves exist was proved in 1888 by the German scientist, Heinrich Hertz, but making use of them was more difficult. In 1896, Guglielmo Marconi managed to send Morse code messages over several kilometres by radio. In 1901, Marconi sent a message 2,000 kilometres across the Atlantic Ocean.

Soon, many ships were fitted with radio equipment to keep in touch with the shore, and a transatlantic radio-telegraph link was set up to link Europe and North America.

Marconi (left) in the radio cabin of his yacht. He is sending a message to the Sydney Radio Exhibition of 1930.

Early broadcast radio

In 1906, American Reginald Aubrey Fessenden discovered that he could use a microphone to make a radio signal change in strength. This meant he could transmit the sound of a person's voice by radio.

Radio broadcasting began in 1921, and by 1925, there were more than 500 radio stations around the world. People listened to the broadcasts on 'crystal' radio sets. Early programmes were mostly music. In many homes, radios became the centrepiece of the sitting room, just as televisions are today. Transistor radios were developed in the 1950s. For the first time, small, cheap, portable radios could be made.

Phone-in radio programmes are popular. The conversation you have with the DJ is broadcast live across the airwaves.

Radio waves

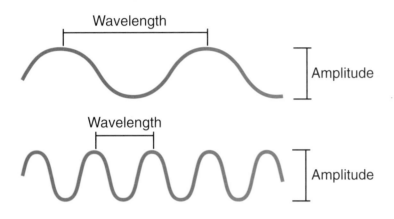

Wavelength

Amplitude

Wavelength

Amplitude

Above **Radio waves are like waves on water. The top wave has the same amplitude as the bottom one, but its wavelength is longer and its frequency is lower.**

Right **A radio station's signal starts out as electrical signals from CD and record players, and the DJ's microphone.**

What are radio waves?

Radio waves make up one part of a range of waves called the electromagnetic spectrum. Light waves and X-rays are also part of the electromagnetic spectrum. Radio waves, just like light waves, travel at the speed of light – almost 300,000 kilometres a second – which is fast enough to circle the world seven times every second.

Amplitude, wavelength and frequency

Radio waves move like the waves in a piece of string when the end of the string is moved up and down quickly. The higher a wave is, the stronger it is. The height is the wave's amplitude. The distance between one wave crest and the next is the wave's wavelength, and the number of wave crests that go past a fixed point each second is the wave's frequency. Wavelength is measured in metres, and frequency in Hertz. As wavelength gets bigger, frequency gets smaller.

How radio waves are made

A radio transmitter is simply a wire with a powerful current of electricity flowing in it. Radio waves are made when the electric current changes strength or direction. Radio waves spread out from the transmitter in all directions.

In a radio studio, the sound of the presenter's voice is turned into an electrical signal by a microphone. This electrical signal is used to change the amplitude of another electrical signal, called the carrier signal. This is called modulation (see page 11). The carrier signal is sent to the transmitter, where it is changed into radio waves, called carrier waves.

Receiving radio waves

When a radio is tuned, the carrier waves for the radio station you want are picked out. The electronic circuits inside the radio change the carrier wave into the carrier signal of the radio station. This signal is very weak, and it must be made bigger, or amplified, before it goes to the loudspeaker to make sound.

A radio mast covered in aerials and transmitters. The dishes send signals in just one direction.

Wavebands

Broadcast radio, police radio, air-traffic control radio, mobile phone communications and so on, all use carrier waves with different wavelengths. For example, most radio stations are on 'medium' wave (MW), which uses wavelengths between 100 metres and 1,000 metres. Using wavebands makes sure that radio signals do not get mixed up.

Who uses radio?

We all do. And often without knowing it. Broadcast radio brings us music, chat shows, comedy shows, sports reports, news, travel and weather reports. You can choose what you want to listen to simply by tuning to the right station.

Local stations give us local news and information about events in our area. They broadcast signals over just a small area. National stations give us national and international news. They broadcast from a network of transmitters over the whole country.

The emergency services arrive quickly at the scene of an accident after a radio call from their base.

Two-way radio

Two-way radio lets two people talk to each other by radio. In remote areas where there are no telephone networks, such as parts of Australia, two-way radio is the only way many people have of staying in touch with each other. In some countries, children talk to their teachers and friends over the radio because they live hundreds of kilometres apart.

Pilots talk to air-traffic controllers, mariners talk to each other and the coastguard, troops talk to their commanders, all by two-way radio. The police, ambulance and fire services all use radio to contact their bases.

What is radio control?

Radio control is a way of controlling a machine from a distance. Radio waves are sent from a hand-held controller to a receiver in the machine. It is used most often for controlling model cars, boats and planes.

Radio in space

Radio is the only way of communicating with spacecraft. It allows astronauts to talk to mission controllers on the Earth. Unmanned spacecraft are controlled by radio signals, and send information to Earth by radio. Even at the speed of light, communication can be slow because of the huge distances. As the space probe *Voyager 2* passed the planet Neptune, signals from it took more than four hours to reach Earth.

The space probe *Voyager 2* sends and receives radio signals with its large communications dish.

Telecommunication links

Radio is also used in the rest of the telecommunications network. TV pictures are broadcast by radio waves (see page 24). Radio waves link mobile phones with fixed transmitting and receiving stations around the countryside (see page 16).

Microwaves are next to radio waves in the electromagnetic spectrum. They can be turned into a narrow beam for sending telephone messages from one transmitter to another (see page 11). Microwaves are also used to send signals to and from communication satellites.

TELEVISION

Early TV programmes

In the 1930s, programmes did not continue all day, and there was only one channel in each country. There were news reports, song and dance shows, and films. All the programmes were live because there was no way of recording pictures. TV allowed people to see live events for the first time.

TV is a way of sending pictures of a moving scene from one place to another. The pictures are converted into an electrical signal by a TV camera. The signals are sent along cables, or by radio waves, to a TV receiver, where they are turned back into pictures on a screen.

Watching TV is easily the most popular form of entertainment in the developed countries of the world. Here, it is unusual for a home not to have a TV set. As well as entertainment, TV brings news and pictures of events around the world, as they happen.

Baird's mechanical television transmitter. The disc with the spiral of holes is called a Nipkow disc.

The pioneer of TV

In 1926, John Logie Baird became the first person to give a demonstration of TV. His system used a mechanical camera, with a big spinning disc. It gave fuzzy and shaky pictures. Baird's system was used for some early TV broadcasts in Britain in the 1930s, but electronic cameras were soon developed which gave clearer and more detailed pictures.

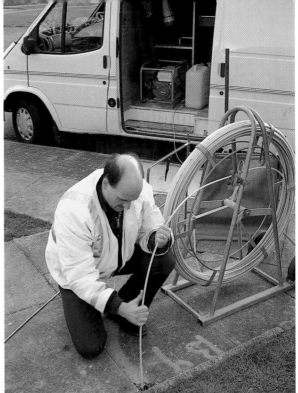

All TV pictures were in black and white until 1953, when the first successful colour pictures were broadcast in the USA. Cable and satellite TV were developed in the 1980s. They gave a greater choice of channels to watch.

With cable television, signals travel along cables instead of through the air. Dozens of channels can travel along the cable at the same time. The cable TV company sends signals from terrestrial TV stations, satellite stations and its own channels, too. Other telecommunication services, such as telephone calls and fax messages, can travel along the same cable.

Satellite and cable TV companies charge a monthly fee for delivering their programmes, and sometimes an extra fee for top sporting action.

Above **A telecommunications engineer feeds an optical-fibre cable for cable TV into a pipe that runs under a customer's garden.**

Left **Maps of streets at the offices of a cable TV company showing cable-laying plans.**

How a TV set works

On a TV screen, you do not really see a moving picture. Instead, you see lots of still pictures one after the other in quick succession. Each picture is slightly different from the one before, and your eyes and brain are fooled into seeing a moving picture. Each still picture is called a frame. It is made up of hundreds of horizontal lines, and each line is made up of hundreds of dots of different colours. You do not see the lines and dots because they all merge together.

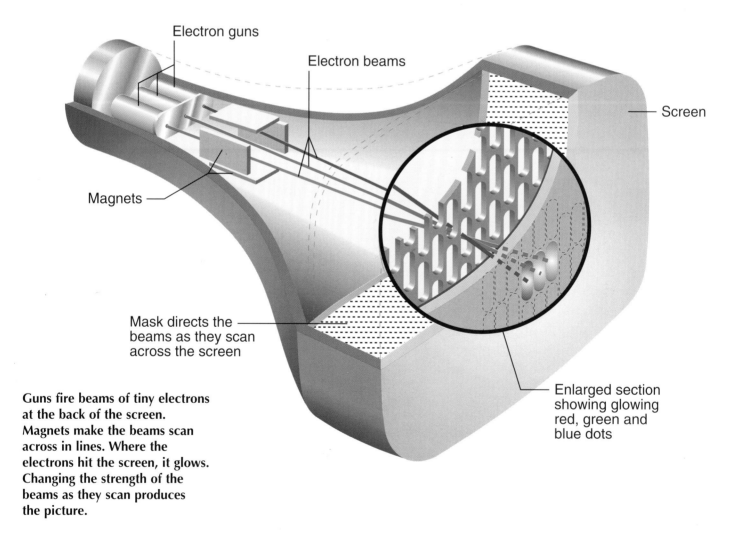

Electron guns

Electron beams

Screen

Magnets

Mask directs the beams as they scan across the screen

Enlarged section showing glowing red, green and blue dots

Guns fire beams of tiny electrons at the back of the screen. Magnets make the beams scan across in lines. Where the electrons hit the screen, it glows. Changing the strength of the beams as they scan produces the picture.

To build a moving picture on the screen, a TV set needs to know the colour of each dot in each line of each frame. It also needs the sound to go with the picture. That is a lot of information. It comes in a continuous signal from the TV company. The signal gets to your set either by radio waves sent from a transmitter to a TV aerial, or by microwaves sent from a satellite to a satellite dish, or along a cable from a cable TV company.

A TV camera filming an outside broadcast. The signals from the camera are relayed to the TV station by a cable, radio or satellite link.

Inside a TV set

Inside a TV set is a long glass tube, called a cathode ray tube, which is like a vase with a thin neck and fat base, laid on its side. The screen is the end of the base. The picture is made by glowing red, green and blue dots behind the screen (they can be seen if the TV screen is looked at closely). The dots are made to glow by tiny particles, called electrons, fired from the other end of the tube. The way the electrons are fired is controlled by the signal which comes from the TV station. Just like a radio, a TV must be tuned to pick up signals from the TV station.

The TV station makes up the signals for your TV. The signals come from TV cameras inside the studio, pictures on outside broadcasts, such as sports events, and from video tape in the studio, which contains signals recorded from the cameras. Computers are used to mix pictures and graphics to create the final pictures that are broadcast.

Why is TV so popular?

TV offers a huge range of programmes to watch. There are entertainment programmes, including cartoons, comedies, dramas, soap operas, films, game shows and sports of many kinds. News reports are broadcast at the same times each day. They bring us up-to-the-minute local, national and international news. Documentary programmes tell us about the world around us, from science to wildlife.

Video cassette recorders (VCRs) are tape recorders for vision and sound signals. They use a magnetic tape in closed plastic cassettes. Educational programmes can be recorded on VCR and shown in classrooms when they are needed.

Portable relay stations use satellites to pass on TV pictures. This one is being used to send pictures of a volcano on a Pacific island to schools in the USA.

Paying for TV

Just as you pay to go to the cinema or to a stadium to watch sport, you have to pay for TV. The money pays for the TV companies to make their programmes. Some countries have a national broadcasting service, which is paid for by buying a licence.

A TV news studio during a broadcast. TV stations contain studios with control rooms that make and transmit programmes.

Most TV companies get their money from advertisers. The advertisers pay money for their products to be shown on TV, but they pass this cost on to their customers by raising the price of the products on sale in the shops. Satellite and cable TV companies might also charge a fee for you to watch feature films and top sporting action.

The number of people who watch different TV programmes, or ratings, is very important to the TV companies and advertisers. Advertisers will pay more to have their advertisements shown during programmes with high ratings, such as popular soap operas and quiz shows.

TV events

Many large events, especially such sporting events as the Olympic Games, are almost controlled by TV companies. The companies will pay huge sums of money to the event organizers for the right to televise the action. Some are watched live by people around the world.

Television companies often have money-raising events for charities and disaster-relief funds, called telethons. TV news pictures of disasters around the world make us more likely to donate our money.

Information on TV

In many areas of the world satellite dishes are the only way of receiving TV broadcasts. These dishes are in Haiti, in the Caribbean.

In some countries you can get written information, such as news, sports results and the weather, on your TV screen. This is called teletext. The information is stored on a computer at the TV station, and is sent page by page along with the TV programme signal. You choose the page you want by pressing buttons on a remote control hand set.

Interactive TV

Interactive TV allows you to send information back to the TV company. One of the most common uses of interactive TV is home shopping, where pictures of goods to buy are shown on TV. Any of the items can be ordered simply by pressing buttons on a special hand set, which is connected to the telephone. The order is sent to the advertisers through the telephone network, who then send the goods to the viewer.

Interactive technology also allows viewers to take part in the programmes themselves. For example, during a quiz programme, viewers can answer questions that appear on the TV screen using the interactive hand set. The viewers can even have a say in the programmes or movies they watch by entering their choice on the handset.

Cable TV stations can offer interactive services easily because information can travel from the viewers along the cable. For example, during a sporting event, signals from all the cameras can be sent, and the viewer can choose between them. With terrestrial and satellite TV, you can send information back to the TV station by telephone.

Many TV companies also offer subtitles or 'closed-captions' for the hearing impaired. They appear along the bottom of the screen. The text is sent along with the pictures and sound for a channel. Sometimes, in addition to the text, there is a person doing sign language in a box in the corner of the screen.

Closed-circuit TV

Closed-circuit TV is the same as normal TV except that the pictures are not broadcast to everybody. Instead, they are sent straight to TV screens watched by security officers. Closed-circuit TV is used in banks, shops, shopping arcades and office blocks. Cameras are positioned to get the best view of the building, and the pictures are recorded in case of a break in.

Above **A closed-circuit security camera mounted on the outside of a building.**

Left **A video studio where pictures from different TV cameras are blended together, or mixed, and made into programmes.**

35

COMPUTER COMMUNICATIONS

An automatic bank teller (ATM) or cashpoint machine talks to the bank's central computer to make sure you have the money you want.

Computer communications allow information to be sent between computers – one computer can receive information from another computer almost anywhere in the world. Every time you buy something in a supermarket, get money from a bank or book a holiday, computers talk to each other. And at work, almost all the computers people use are linked to other computers in the company.

How computers talk to each other

Inside a computer, information is stored in digital form (see panel). Information, such as a page of words, is made up of many thousands of digits. It is sent from one computer along one wire, one digit after another.

Computers in different offices are connected through the telecommunications network. To do this, each computer needs a special electronic device, called a modem. It changes the digital information into an electrical signal which can travel through the network. When the signal arrives, it is turned back into digital form.

Digital information

Digital information is information in binary numbers. Binary numbers have just the digits 0 and 1. These are easy for a computer to store and send in electrical form by turning a current on for 1 and off for 0. Combinations of 0s and 1s can represent any sort of information, such as dates, names, pages of words, pictures and sounds.

All the computers in this office are linked to computers in other offices through the telephone network.

The speed that a modem sends or receives information is measured in bits per second. The fastest ones can send over 28,000 bits per second – enough to send all the words in this book in two seconds.

Companies who use computer communications all the time use special digital telephone lines, called ISDN lines, which do not need modems. Information can be sent along them much more quickly. With a portable computer and a mobile phone, you can send information from almost anywhere.

Computer communications history

Businesses began using computers widely in the 1960s. If computers needed to communicate with each other, they did it along special cables. Personal computers became available in the early 1980s. They could talk over the telephone with a device called an acoustic coupler. Soon after this, modems were developed. As the cost of modems and telephone calls has become cheaper, computer communications has become popular.

Computer networks

The operations room of a telecommunications centre. The computers control and monitor the communications passing through the centre.

A computer network is made up of computers that can exchange information. It can contain just two computers, dozens of computers or many thousands of computers. A local-area network (LAN) links up computers in the same room or building. A wide-area network (WAN) links computers in different buildings, towns and cities, or even countries. Computers in a WAN are linked through the telecommunications network.

Video conferencing

With videoconferencing equipment, two people on a computer network can talk each other, and see each other at the same time. Each computer needs a microphone and a small video camera. The voices and pictures are turned into digital information and then sent over the network.

The people in this videoconference can see and talk to the person on the screen. She can also see them on a screen in her office.

Who uses networks?

Almost all of us, even though we might not know it. In offices, people use LANs to share computer resources, such as printers. Companies such as large supermarket chains and banks use networks to link together all their branches and offices.

Many people are teleworkers. They work on computers at their homes, using information sent along the telephone line from their company's computers.

E-mail

E-mail is short for electronic mail. It is a way of sending messages over a computer network. One person on the network writes a message, gives the computer the 'address' of the other computer and presses a button to send it. Almost instantly, it arrives at the other computer, where the other person can read it. It is much quicker than sending the same message by post.

The Internet

The Internet (or just the 'Net') is the world's biggest computer network. It stretches right around the world, and links together many millions of computer users. The Internet is really a huge network of smaller networks linked together.

Anybody with a personal computer and a modem can join the Internet. The computers on the Internet are linked together through the telecommunications network and with dedicated digital links.

A computer linked to the Internet at a 'cyber cafe'. Visitors with little computer knowledge can 'surf the Net' using just a mouse.

The Internet is a supernetwork of computers. With it you can receive words, pictures and sounds from computers all over the world.

The Internet grew from a computer network that was set up in the 1960s, which linked together military supercomputers in the USA. People using it began sending each other e-mail and the idea caught on. Its rapid expansion in the 1990s is due largely to the availability of cheap personal computers.

Using the Internet

On the Internet, you can send e-mail to other users, find all types of information on thousands of different subjects, hold conversations on your screen with groups of users and transfer information to other computers.

The Internet is a very fast and efficient way of passing information around the world. The number of people and companies who are connected to it is increasing at an amazing rate, and huge amounts of information are sent around it every minute of every day.

The World Wide Web

The 'Web' is the fastest growing area of the Internet. It allows you to look at information stored on Web sites on the Internet. The information at a Web site can be text, pictures, sounds and video clips, or a mixture of all of these. An increasing number of organizations are publishing information on the Web. For example, your favourite sports team probably has a Web site, giving information about the team's games and general gossip about the players.

THE FUTURE

A technician adjusts a picture on a high-definition TV (HDTV). An HDTV screen is made up of 1,125 horizontal lines, and is wider than a normal TV screen.

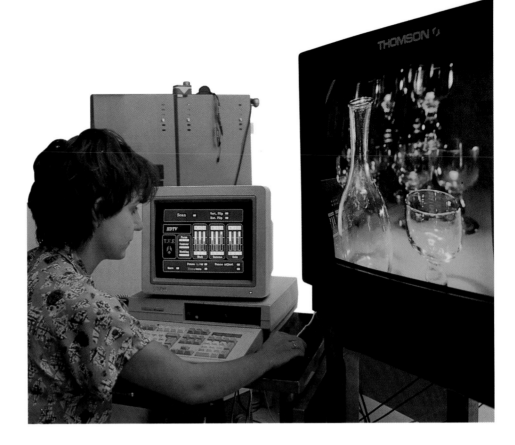

The future for telecommunications is exciting. Personal communication machines will be available, able to work anywhere on Earth, sending signals to orbiting satellites. TV pictures will be much more detailed than they are today – they might even be three dimensional – and there will be hundreds of channels to choose from. All your communications by telephone, television and computer will travel along the same route (via satellite or cable) to your home.

The telecommunications network will become more 'intelligent'. You will have a personal telephone number, and the network will be able to track you down, wherever you are, to give you your call. All information will travel everywhere in digital form.

What will telephones and TV look like?

At home, you might need just one machine for all your communications. You will have a cross between a TV and a computer. It will receive TV programmes and act as a computer, receiving information from the Internet. It could also act as a video telephone. And it is likely to be flat, like a large picture hanging on the wall.

While you are out, you will carry a personal digital assistant (PDA). It will be a telephone, digital diary and address book, fax machine and computer, all rolled into one, and the size of your palm.

Instant access

In the future, you will have instant access to any information and entertainment you want, wherever you are. It will not make your life much different – just more convenient. You will be able to shop from home in virtual shopping centres or watch any film 'on demand'.

Better long-distance communications will mean fewer hours wasted travelling around. You might never need to leave home. But imagine how boring the world would be if nobody went out and talked to each other face-to-face.

Above **This road-side telephone in northern Spain is solar powered and communicates by radio. The solar panel and aerial are on top of the mast.**

Left **A computerized telephone customer service centre with a videoconferencing link.**

DATE CHART

1845 Samuel Morse opens the first telegraph line in the USA, stretching from Washington to Baltimore.

1866 The ship, the *Great Eastern*, successfully lays a submarine telegraph cable under the Atlantic Ocean, from Valentia in Ireland to Newfoundland in Canada.

1876 Alexander Graham Bell demonstrates the first working telephone receiver at the Centennial Exhibition in Philadelphia in the USA.

1878 The first telephone exchange, with twenty-one subscribers, opens in New Haven in Connecticut in the USA.

1878 Edison invents a microphone that greatly improves the working of the telephone.

1888 German physicist Heinrich Hertz carries out experiments which prove the existence of radio waves.

1891 William Gray of Hartford in the USA forms the Gray Telephone Pay Station Company, which rents out coin-box public telephones to be used in shops.

1896 In London, Italian radio pioneer Guglielmo Marconi demonstrates his radio telegraph system to the Post Office.

1901 Guglielmo Marconi succeeds in transmitting the letter 's' in Morse code by radio telegraph across the Atlantic, from England to Newfoundland in Canada.

1906 Canadian scientist Reginald Fessenden, who worked out a way of sending sounds by radio, makes the first radio broadcast, made up of music, songs and poems.

1907 In Germany, a photograph is sent along a telephone line between Munich and Berlin. It is the first fax transmission.

1925 The first radio stations are broadcasting in the USA and Europe.

1926 The first working TV system, which uses a mechanical camera and receiver, is demonstrated in London by Scotsman John Logie Baird.

1927 A radio-telephone link is set up between Europe and North America so that telephone subscribers in different continents can talk to each other.

1932 The first regular TV programmes are broadcast from London by the BBC, using John Logie Baird's mechanical television system.

1953 In the USA, colour TV broadcasts, which can also be received on black-and-white TVs, begin.

1955 The small Sony TR-55 becomes the first transistor radio available for people to buy.

1956 The first submarine telephone cable, which can carry nearly 600 telephone calls at the same time, is laid under the Atlantic Ocean.

1956 The first use of videotape to record TV programmes.

1962 The US National Aeronautics and Space Administration (NASA) launches *Telstar*, the first communications satellite, which can relay sixty telephone calls or one TV channel.

1966 Two scientists at the Standard Telephone Company discover that a glass fibre can carry much more information then an electrical current in a wire.

1969 Four powerful supercomputers at US defence sites are connected together to form a computer network called the DARPANET. It is the start of the Internet.

1970 The first optical fibres suitable for long-range communication are manufactured.

1977 The world's first optical-fibre telephone link is opened in the USA.

1979 The Swedish company Ericsson builds a mobile phone network, allowing people to use mobile phones for the first time.

1981 Computer manufacturer IBM launches its first microcomputer, the IBM PC. Most personal computers have grown from this design.

1986 The first Direct Broadcasting Satellite (DBS) goes into operation. It beamed signals direct to dishes on individual houses.

1987 The Apple Macintosh II home computer sets new standards for power and ease of use.

1988 An optical-fibre cable able to carry telephone calls, TV pictures and computer data is laid between the USA, Britain and France.

1989 An optical-fibre cable is laid across the Pacific Ocean.

GLOSSARY

aerial A device which sends out and/or receives radio signals. Aerials can be a single wire or a dish.

air-traffic controllers People who ensure that aircraft stay clear of each other while in the air.

bit In computing, a bit is the smallest piece of information possible. It is either 0 or 1. Computers store every sort of information in combinations of bits.

broadcast To send information, such as radio or television signals, so that they can be received by anybody with a suitable receiver.

crystal radio sets Early types of radio sets with a crystal for demodulating radio signals.

dedicated Allocated to do a particular thing.

electric current A flow of electricity. An electric current is made up of particles called electrons moving along, normally in a wire.

electrical signal An electric current which changes in strength and direction. The changes represent information, such as the shape of a sound wave.

electromagnetic spectrum The whole family of related electromagnetic waves. Radio waves, microwaves, light, X-rays, and infra-red waves are all members of the electromagnetic spectrum.

graphics Pictures which appear on a computer screen, or which are produced by a computer.

ground station A transmitter or receiver on the Earth's surface which sends signals to or receives them from a satellite.

interactive movie A film which has several different plots. The plot you see depends on decisions you make about the characters during the film.

loudspeaker A device which turns an electrical signal into the sound represented by the signal.

microphone A device which turns a sound into an electrical signal.

microwave A type of radio wave which is part of the electromagnetic spectrum.

modulation Using an electrical signal to change the shape of a radio wave or light wave.

network Two or more computers or other communication machines linked together so that they can exchange information.

optical fibre A thin thread of glass or plastic inside which light travels. The light does not escape even when the fibre is bent.

outside broadcast A TV or radio programme made away from the station's studio. Most outside broadcasts are made at sporting events.

radio-telegraph A telegraph machine which sends its electrical code by radio instead of along wires.

receiver A machine which detects telecommunication signals (telephone calls, radio or TV signals) and turns them back into their original form.

satellite A machine which orbits the Earth. Telecommunication satellites relay signals around the Earth.

satellite dish A dish-shaped aerial which collects radio signals. A dish can detect a weaker signal than an aerial made with a straight wire.

sensor A device that detects changes in light, temperature or pressure, and turns them into an electrical signal.

space probe A spacecraft which travels to planets or other objects in space to investigate them.

supercomputer The most powerful (capable of carrying out calculations the fastest) sort of computer. Supercomputers are used for complex scientific research.

terrestrial Of the land. Terrestrial TV companies send their signals over the Earth's surface from a transmitter on land, rather than by satellite.

transistor An electronic device that can amplify (make bigger) an electrical signal, or act as a switch, turning an electric current on or off. Transistors are used in most communication equipment and all computers.

transmitter A device which sends out a telecommunications signal (telephone calls, radio or TV).

video tape Plastic tape covered in magnetic material on to which a video signal (an electrical signal representing a TV picture) can be recorded as a magnetic pattern.

FIND OUT MORE

Books to read

Communications by Nigel Hawkes (Watts, 1994)
Communications Through Time by Chris Oxlade (Macdonald Young Books, 1996)
Language and Communications by Neil Ardley (Watts, 1989)
Satellites by Steve Parker (Wayland, 1996)
The Internet by Robert Snedden (Wayland, 1997)

Places to visit

Museum of Communication, University of Edinburgh, Mayfield Road, Edinburgh
A collection of devices used in telecommunications, including telephones, radios, transmitters, televisions and teleprinters.

The National Museum of Film, Photography and Television, Bradford
Includes exhibits about the history of TV, and a working TV studio.

The Science Museum, Exhibition Road, London
Many exhibits about radio, TV, telephones and the telegraph.

INDEX

48